CW01497396

PARAGUAY TR GUIDE FOR BEGINNERS

The Updated Concise Guide for Planning a Trip to Paraguay Including Top Destinations,Culture,Outdoor Adventures,Cuisine and Getting Around

Nicolash Enzo
Copyright@2023

TABLE OF CONTENT

CHAPTER 1

INTRODUCTION

Located in the central region of South America, Paraguay is a landlocked country renowned for its diverse cultural heritage, historical significance, and abundant natural landscapes. Despite its comparatively small dimensions, this nation has a certain charm that enthralls the inquisitive voyager. Paraguay's geographical position, with Argentina to the south and southwest, Brazil to the east and northeast, and Bolivia to the northwest, renders it a pivotal junction of many influences. Consequently, its strategic location engenders a compelling amalgamation of customs and a discernible way of life.

Geographical diversity and landscape are significant factors that contribute to the overall understanding and analysis of a certain region or area.

The scenery of Paraguay is characterized by a harmonious combination of undulating hills, fertile plains, and winding rivers, resulting in a captivating and visually appealing panorama. The Paraguay River, an essential conduit for the nation, meanders across the central region of the country, establishing connections between important urban centers and providing a picturesque setting for several notable locations. The Gran Chaco, an extensive lowland plain that spans the western portion of the nation, presents a notable juxtaposition to the rich plains found in the eastern section. Within this location, one may see a distinctive ecosystem characterized by a high level of biodiversity, where the natural cycles of the environment play a prominent role.

The concept of a cultural melting pot refers to a society or community where individuals from many cultural backgrounds come together and contribute to the formation of a new, blended

Paraguay's culture is characterized by a dynamic amalgamation of indigenous heritage and European influences, resulting in a captivating tapestry that narrates a fascinating narrative. The Guarani, an indigenous community that has a significant presence, has had a profound impact on the national identity of Paraguay. Their language, customs, and way of life have been intricately intertwined within the social fabric of Paraguayan society. The cultural fabric of the region is enhanced by the presence of Spanish colonial legacy, which is shown via the architectural structures, religious customs, and historical locations that are scattered across the area.

The concept of historical significance refers to the assessment of the importance and impact of events, individuals, or developments in the past. It

The history of Paraguay is characterized by a multifaceted account of achievements and difficulties, as well as the ability to endure and make advancements. The discussion of Paraguay necessitates an acknowledgment of the significant influence exerted by the Triple Alliance War (1864-1870), a military confrontation that fundamentally altered the course of the country's development. The enduring impact of the conflict is evident in the tangible remnants of historical places and monuments, serving as poignant symbols that commemorate the profound sacrifices undertaken. However, from this challenging experience, a sense of cohesion and resilience arose, which still characterizes the people of Paraguay in the present day.

Traditional Cuisine and Culinary Delights

A comprehensive study of Paraguay would be considered incomplete without partaking in its unique culinary offerings. Paraguayan cuisine showcases the amalgamation of indigenous and European gastronomic customs, yielding a diverse and palatable assortment of tastes. One might indulge in the pleasurable experience of chipa, a bread characterized by its cheesiness and chewy texture, crafted from manioc flour. Alternatively, one can delight in the opulent taste profiles offered by sopa paraguaya, a meal consisting of cornbread infused with cheese. One should not overlook the opportunity to partake in the sociable atmosphere of a customary asado, a culinary event that unites kin and companions in the enjoyment of a delectable assortment of grilled meats.

The concept of warmth and hospitality is a fundamental aspect of human interaction and has been widely recognized as an important cultural value across all societies.

The lasting impression that tourists often retain from their experience in Paraguay is the notable kindness shown by its inhabitants. Paraguayans are renowned for their hospitable nature and genuine friendliness, fostering an inclusive atmosphere that ensures a warm welcome for all visitors. Engaging in dialogues with local residents is a prevalent practice among travelers, as it offers an opportunity to get firsthand knowledge about their cultural practices and lifestyle, so enhancing the authenticity and depth of the trip experience.

Distinctive Festivals and Celebrations

Paraguay's calendar is replete with exuberant festivals and festivities that serve as a manifestation of its multifaceted cultural history. The Carnaval de Encarnación, renowned for its popularity, attracts a multitude of spectators from both local and distant regions who gather to see vibrant processions, lively melodies, and spirited choreography. Semana Santa, also known as Holy Week, is a period characterized by profound religious devotion in Paraguay. During this time, the country engages in processions and rituals that provide valuable insights into Paraguay's spiritual identity.

The preservation of tradition is a significant aspect of cultural heritage that plays a crucial role in maintaining the identity and continuity of societies.

Paraguay has a notable inclination towards the preservation and reverence of tradition, with its acceptance of modernity. Artisanal workmanship flourishes, giving rise to elaborate creations such as ñandutí lace and ao po'i fabrics, both of which are esteemed manifestations of creative expression. The aforementioned crafts not only serve as a demonstration of the exceptional craftsmanship possessed by Paraguayan artists, but also encapsulate the narratives and heritages that have been transmitted over successive generations.

Paraguay, sometimes eclipsed by its more sizable neighboring countries, serves as a testimony to the aesthetic appeal of underappreciated regions. The scenery, culture, and history of this place intertwine to create a tale that is both enthralling and humbling. While exploring the picturesque streets of Asunción, contemplating the expansive Chaco region, or indulging in the harmonious melodies of Paraguayan harp music, one cannot help but develop a profound appreciation for the intrinsic qualities of this modest country. Paraguay serves as a remarkable example of a nation where various elements converge to create a complex and captivating cultural fabric that is distinctly Paraguayan.

CHAPTER 2

Getting to Paraguay

Imagine embarking on a voyage that transports you to the core of South America, a region teeming with a rich tapestry of cultural multiplicity, awe-inspiring natural phenomena, and profound historical significance. The attractiveness of Paraguay lies in its potential for exploration by those with an adventurous disposition and a penchant for the exceptional. In anticipation of commencing this exhilarating journey, acquiring a comprehensive comprehension of the intricacies involved in reaching Paraguay emerges as a crucial undertaking, therefore guaranteeing a seamless and intellectually rewarding travel endeavor.

Navigating the requirements for admission

Prior to embarking on a journey to Paraguay, it is important to possess a comprehensive understanding of the admission restrictions imposed by the nation. Paraguay has a somewhat permissive attitude towards foreign tourists; nonetheless, the specific admission procedures may differ based on one's nationality. Several nations, such as the United States, Canada, and other European countries, have implemented a policy whereby individuals engaging in tourist activities are not obligated to get a visa for a duration of up to 90 days. Nevertheless, it is recommended to verify the current entrance requirements and any potential modifications by contacting the Paraguayan consulate or embassy in one's place of residence.

Determining the Ideal Timing for a Visit

The climate of Paraguay exhibits discernible wet and dry seasons, exerting a notable impact on the optimal periods for visiting the country. The dry season, which typically extends from May to September, is often regarded as the optimal period for tourists due to its favorable climatic conditions characterized by comfortable warmth, limited precipitation, and unobstructed opportunities for outdoor activities. Nevertheless, it is important to acknowledge that the natural splendor of Paraguay is most prominent during the wet season, spanning from October to April. It is during this period that the verdant landscapes come alive, adorned with vivid hues and teeming with flourishing flora and wildlife.

The topic of discussion pertains to airports and transportation.

The Silvio Pettirossi foreign Airport in Asunción functions as the principal point of entry for foreign visitors embarking on their journey to Paraguay. The contemporary airport provides a variety of facilities and services, so providing a seamless and pleasant transition for travelers entering the nation. Asunción, the capital city of Paraguay, benefits from the availability of air travel links offered by several international airlines. This facilitates relatively convenient access to Asunción from major cities throughout the globe.

Upon arrival, a variety of ground transportation alternatives are easily accessible to facilitate travel to one's desired location inside the country of Paraguay. Taxis and ride-sharing services are seen as practical transportation options, and it is advisable to possess the local money, namely the Paraguayan Guarani, for the purpose of remuneration. Furthermore, automobile rental services provide individuals with the opportunity to independently tour the nation at their own speed, and prominent rental businesses conveniently operate at airport locations.

Navigating the procedures related to visas and customs.

The completion of immigration and customs formalities is a customary aspect of foreign travel, and Paraguay adheres to this practice. Upon arrival, individuals will go through the process of immigration check, during which their passports will be stamped and their entrance data will be duly documented. It is essential to guarantee that one's passport remains valid for a minimum of six months beyond the desired departure date from Paraguay.

Customs rules often exhibit a high degree of clarity, whereby individuals are obligated to disclose any things that are subject to duty or limitations. It is recommended that individuals acquaint themselves with the particular customs restrictions of Paraguay before to their arrival, particularly if they want to import items such as electronics, alcohol, or tobacco products. This will aid in the prevention of unforeseen circumstances and guarantee a seamless procedure of entrance.

Strategies for an Effortless Arrival

The first aspect to consider is documentation. It is advisable to ensure that all essential papers, including the passport, return ticket, and any requisite visas, are easily accessible and well-arranged.

2. Acquisition of Local Currency: It is advisable to get a certain amount of local currency upon arrival in order to cover initial expenditures such as transportation, food, and incidental costs.

The topic of communication is of great significance in several academic disciplines. For those who do not possess fluency in the Spanish language, it is advisable to acquire a rudimentary understanding of key terms or use a translation application to enhance the ease of communication.

4. Health Considerations: It is advisable to inquire about the recommended or

mandatory vaccines and health measures before to embarking on a trip to Paraguay.

5. Accommodation: It is advisable to include the necessary information pertaining to your accommodation, such as the address and contact details, while completing the immigration form.

6. Contact Information for Emergencies: It is advisable to have a comprehensive record of emergency contacts, which should include the relevant embassy or consulate of one's home country in Paraguay.

Embarking upon a sojourn to Paraguay presents a unique prospect to deeply engage with a riveting amalgamation of historical narratives, cultural expressions, and awe-inspiring natural landscapes.

Ensuring a flawless arrival and setting the tone for a great journey involves effectively navigating the complexities of entrance rules, transportation, and procedures. By adequately preparing, one will discover a nation that accepts variety and invites others to uncover its hidden wonders.

CHAPTER 3

Exploring Paraguay's Top Destinations

Located in the central region of South America, Paraguay entices tourists with its diverse blend of cultural legacy, historical importance, and remarkable natural attractions. With its diverse range of locations, including both vibrant urban centers and secluded natural landscapes, this nation has a multitude of sites that have the potential to fascinate and evoke inspiration. As one embarks on a tour around the prominent attractions of Paraguay, they may anticipate being fully immersed in a rich assortment of encounters that reveal the fundamental nature of this captivating territory.

1. Asunción: A Study of the Capital's Charms and Cultural Offerings

The capital city of Asunción in Paraguay acts as a dynamic representation of the country's historical and modern aspects. The juxtaposition of colonial buildings and modern innovations in this context serves as a visual representation of the complex interrelationship between historical and contemporary elements. Commence your trip by embarking on a visit to the esteemed city center, renowned for its historical significance. Within this locale, one will encounter notable structures like as the Palacio de los López, which serves as the presidential palace. This architectural masterpiece exemplifies the refined neoclassical aesthetic and serves as a poignant representation of Paraguay's indomitable resilience.

Explore the historical aspects of Asunción further by visiting the Museo del Barro, an institution devoted to the conservation and exhibition of indigenous and traditional art. In this exposition, readers will get a comprehensive understanding of the Guarani culture, a cultural phenomenon that has had a profound impact on the formation and development of Paraguay's national identity. In order to indulge in the regional gastronomy, one can consider visiting the Mercado Cuatro, a vibrant marketplace that offers an opportunity to partake in authentic Paraguayan cuisine such as chipa, a kind of cheese bread, while immersing oneself in the daily cadence of local life.

2. Ciudad del Este: A Vibrant Border Town with Scenic Splendor

Situated on the border with Brazil, Ciudad del Este is recognized as a prominent commercial center renowned for its vibrant markets, varied retail options, and close proximity to the remarkable Itaipu Dam. The urban marketplaces inside the city, such as the Mercado de Abasto, exhibit a diverse range of commodities, including electronics and textiles, therefore drawing in customers from far locations. One may see the cosmopolitan amalgamation of many cultures and the dynamic liveliness that defines this border town by leisurely traversing around its bustling marketplaces.

Located in close proximity to Ciudad del Este, the Itaipu Dam stands as an impressive testament to human engineering prowess, ranking among the biggest hydroelectric dams worldwide. Participate on a guided tour to get knowledge about the engineering marvels of the dam and its consequential effects on

Paraguay's electricity output. When in the vicinity, it is advisable to see the captivating Iguazu Falls, an esteemed UNESCO World Heritage Site situated on the border shared by Argentina and Brazil. Experience the formidable force of nature as water gracefully descends over verdant precipices in a captivating exhibition.

3. Encarnación: A Comprehensive Exploration of Carnival Festivities and Historical Significance

Encarnación, situated next to the Paraná River, is renowned for its exuberant Carnaval de Encarnación, a vivid commemoration that highlights the country's profound affinity for song, dancing, and revelry. The yearly occurrence of this event results in a vibrant display of parades, costumes, and rhythmic performances, attracting tourists from many locations within the vicinity.

In addition to its vibrant carnival, the city of Encarnación has significant historical assets, notably the Jesuit missions, which provide valuable insights into Paraguay's colonial history. The Jesús de Tavarangue and the Santísima Trinidad de Paraná are architectural remains that have been recognized by UNESCO, serving as tangible evidence of the historical impact made by Jesuit missionaries in the area. While engaging with these historical locations, one is encouraged to envision the resonance of bygone eras resonating inside the solid confines of the stone structures.

4. Ybycuí National Park: Exploring the Wilderness and Gaining Cultural Understanding

Ybycuí National Park is an enticing opportunity for anyone in search of outdoor pursuits and a more profound communion with the natural world. The designated region serves as a sanctuary for a wide range of biological variety, characterized by densely populated woodlands, cascading water formations, and a varied array of animal species. Engage in the exploration of hiking pathways that meander through the park, giving individuals the chance to experience distinctive plant and animal species while immersing themselves in the tranquility of the environment.

Ybycuí National Park offers valuable insights into the Guarani legacy due to the presence of indigenous settlements in close proximity to the park. Interact with the Guarani community in order to get knowledge about their cultural practices, societal norms, and deep-rooted relationship with the natural environment. The inclusion of this cultural exchange enhances the experiential aspect of your journey, facilitating a deeper understanding of the interdependent connection between human societies and the natural environment.

The Chaco Region: An Exploration of Untamed Nature and Indigenous Interactions

The Chaco Region, which spans the western territory of Paraguay, is characterized by its pristine natural environment and the presence of indigenous communities. This expansive and sparsely inhabited region provides adventurous explorers with a chance to immerse themselves in the essence of

Paraguay's natural environments and establish connections with isolated people.

The Chaco region has a diverse range of animals, including as jaguars, tapirs, and capybaras, making it an appealing destination for those with a keen interest in wildlife. Engaging in the activity of birdwatching may be quite gratifying, especially within the confines of the Gran Chaco Americano Biosphere Reserve, which has a remarkable diversity of more than 500 avian species. Guided excursions give valuable insights into the ecological importance of the area and present opportunities for seeing secretive fauna.

The Chaco region is inhabited by indigenous populations like as the Enxet and Ayoreo, who have successfully preserved their ancient way of life within the natural environment. Interacting with these tribes provides an opportunity to get insights into their cultural practices, traditional beliefs, and profound attachment to the natural environment. This initiative provides a platform for the sharing of cultural experiences, which facilitates the development of mutual understanding and appreciation.

The many places in Paraguay together provide a diverse range of experiences that effectively showcase the complex nature of the country. Paraguay's cultural heritage, natural beauty, and historical significance can be explored through various destinations within the country. These include the dynamic capital of Asunción, the captivating Carnaval de Encarnación, the wilderness of Ybycuí National Park, and the untamed landscapes of the Chaco region. Each of these locations provides a distinct perspective on Paraguay's rich offerings. While exploring the various terrains and interacting with the inhabitants residing inside them, individuals will get fully immersed in a voyage of exploration that enhances their comprehension of this captivating country situated in South America.

CHAPTER 4

Unforgettable Activities and Experiences in Paraguay

Paraguay, a nation characterized by a convergence of many cultures, captivating historical narratives, and remarkable natural wonders, presents an array of opportunities and encounters that have the potential to enhance the voyager's expedition. With its diverse range of experiences, South America offers a multitude of opportunities for individuals to engage in cultural immersion via traditional music, culinary exploration, market visits, and wilderness expeditions. This continent presents a rich tapestry of choices that appeal to a wide array of tastes and interests. As one traverses the intricate web of personal encounters, it is essential to anticipate the formation of enduring recollections that reveal the fundamental nature of Paraguay.

One aspect of cultural expression that has significant value is the performance of traditional music and dance.

The cultural essence of Paraguay is vividly expressed via its music and dance, offering a profound sensory experience that delves into the very core of the nation's collective identity. The evocative harmonies produced by the harp, guitar, and folk instruments serve as a means of narrative expression, recounting tales pertaining to themes of affection, historical events, and the mundane aspects of existence. The experience of seeing live renditions of classic Paraguayan musical genres, such as the polka and guarania, provides a deep and meaningful link to the cultural legacy of the region.

To fully engage in an authentic and all-encompassing encounter, it is advisable to contemplate participating in nearby festivals and communal festivities. The Carnaval de Encarnación is a vibrant celebration that highlights the lively essence of the country via its flamboyant parades and rhythmic dances. To really immerse oneself in the cultural essence of Paraguay, it is advisable to actively interact with the local population and actively participate in the many celebratory events. By doing so, one may genuinely experience the vibrant energy and spirit of Paraguay, which will undoubtedly leave a lasting impression.

2. Paraguayan Gastronomy and Culinary Experiences:

Partaking in Paraguayan gastronomy is a fundamental aspect of one's voyage, providing a captivating study of tastes that embody the country's many cultural influences. Chipa, a kind of cheese bread derived from manioc flour, is often consumed with meals and is highly regarded as a popular snack. Indulge in sopa paraguaya, a delectable culinary creation consisting of cornbread and cheese, renowned for its ability to provide solace and a sense of coziness.

In order to have a comprehensive understanding of the culinary landscape, it is advisable to engage in the exploration of indigenous marketplaces and dining establishments. Mercado Cuatro, located in Asunción, has a diverse selection of street food vendors that provide a wide range of delectable offerings, including empanadas and pastries. It is advisable to contemplate enrolling in a culinary course with the intention of acquiring the skills necessary to proficiently craft these customary gastronomic delights, so facilitating the replication of Paraguayan flavors inside the confines of one's own domicile.

In the context of acquiring crafts and souvenirs, the act of shopping is a common practice. This activity involves the exploration and selection of various items that are often associated with cultural or artistic significance. The purpose of engaging in this endeavor is to get tangible objects that serve as memories

The act of visiting local markets not only provides a sensory experience but also presents an occasion to contribute to the livelihood of local craftspeople and acquire distinctive mementos. The marketplaces in Paraguay exhibit a diverse assortment of merchandise, including handcrafted fabrics and intricately designed lacework. Ñandutí lace and ao po'i textiles are two notable examples of Paraguayan workmanship that exhibit elaborate designs. These exquisite creations serve as thoughtful presents and cherished mementos.

Mercado 4, located in Ciudad del Este, is a vibrant marketplace renowned for its diverse range of merchandise, including both modern gadgets and old artisanal products. Interacting with suppliers facilitates a deeper understanding of their expertise and narratives, enabling the establishment of meaningful relationships that extend beyond just commercial transactions.

The topic of interest is Outdoor Adventures and Nature Exploration.

The various landscapes of Paraguay attract explorers with a wide range of outdoor sports. Ybycuí National Park has a remarkable natural landscape characterized by its lush woods and cascading waterfalls. The park boasts a network of hiking routes that guide visitors to awe-inspiring vantage spots, while also providing many possibilities for engaging in the activity of birding. In contrast, the Chaco Region provides opportunities for immersive experiences in the environment, allowing visitors to engage in activities such as animal observation and birdwatching, which reveal the region's abundant natural diversity.

To enhance one's experience, one may participate in horseback riding expeditions that provide a unique vantage point of the rural landscapes of Paraguay. Pampas, wetland ecosystems distinguished by abundant grasses and meandering water channels, provide an optimal environment for engaging in this particular endeavor, facilitating a profound connection with the natural world as one traverses through visually captivating terrains.

One aspect of our program is the inclusion of cultural workshops and immersion experiences.

Gain a more comprehensive understanding of Paraguayan culture via active engagement in seminars and immersive experiences. Acquire proficiency in playing classical musical instruments such as the harp or guitar, or participate in artisanal classes aimed at crafting intricate ñandutí lace or ao po'i fabrics. These activities not only provide practical experiences but also cultivate an admiration for the skill and commitment that characterize Paraguayan workmanship.

One more approach of fully experiencing Paraguay's culture is by active involvement with local populations. Homestays with indigenous families in the Chaco Region provide an opportunity to obtain valuable insights into their cultural practices and lifestyle. By actively engaging in everyday activities and immersing oneself in their traditions, participants may get a deep knowledge of their way of life.

In this section, we will discuss religious festivals and celebrations.

The religious festivals of Paraguay provide an insight into the spiritual and cultural aspects of the country. Semana Santa, often known as Holy Week, is a culturally and religiously important period characterized by a series of processions, ceremonies, and reenactments that commemorate biblical events. During this week, community members gather to engage in introspection over their religious beliefs and participate in longstanding cultural customs.

Participating in these events not only provides an opportunity to get insight into Paraguayan spirituality, but also enables one to see the cohesive nature and profound dedication of the community.

Interacting with indigenous people during these festivities cultivates a more profound affiliation with the socio-cultural tapestry of the country.

As one embarks on a trip through the many activities and experiences offered in Paraguay, a multifaceted country, they will have the opportunity to unveil the intricate layers that contribute to its unique character. The many cultural experiences in Paraguay, ranging from the melodic tunes of traditional music to the flavorful culinary offerings of Paraguayan cuisine, as well as the exploration of vibrant marketplaces and the immersion into the unspoiled wilderness, all contribute to the comprehensive depiction of Paraguay. One should eagerly seize the chance to actively participate in interactions with nearby people, deeply involve oneself in longstanding customs, and establish meaningful relationships that will last far after the conclusion of the expedition. Paraguay has a diverse range of opportunities for anyone seeking cultural enrichment, outdoor adventure, or an authentic view of daily living. These experiences are known to deeply resonate with individuals, leaving a lasting impact on their emotional and spiritual well-being.

CHAPTER 5

Cultural Insights of Paraguay

Paraguay, situated in the central region of South America, is renowned for its abundant cultural variety. This nation serves as a captivating example of the intricate interplay between indigenous heritage and colonial legacies, resulting in a distinctive mosaic of customs, artistic expressions, and enduring societal practices that have withstood the test of time. As one embarks on a journey to investigate the cultural nuances of Paraguay, they will become fully engrossed in a realm where archaic beliefs harmoniously coexist with contemporary elements, where elaborate handicrafts serve as conduits for ancestral narratives, and where ceremonial practices and festivities serve as manifestations of the nation's profound sense of collective identity and cohesion.

1. The Guarani Heritage: A Continuously Evolving Legacy

The cultural environment of Paraguay is significantly shaped by the legacy of the Guarani people, who constitute one of the most prominent indigenous communities inside the nation. The Guarani people have significantly impacted Paraguayan culture, exerting influence on several aspects such as language, rituals, and cognitive frameworks. The Guarani language, in conjunction with Spanish, has the status of an official language in Paraguay, reflecting the country's dedication to the preservation of its indigenous heritage.

In addition to linguistic aspects, the cultural traditions and belief systems of the Guarani people persist and flourish. The Guarani way of life highlights the great interconnection between people and their environment, shown in their strong spiritual bond with the land and wildlife, as well as their distinctive cosmology. Interacting with Guarani villages provides an opportunity to get insight into their cultural milieu, enabling one to see their rich artistic creations, oral traditions, and ceremonial practices that have been transmitted over several generations.

2. The Intersection of Folk Art and Craftsmanship: Narrative Weaving via Threads

The artistic tradition of Paraguay is expressed via its elaborate craftsmanship, with each individual work reflecting the influence of cultural legacy and hereditary knowledge. Ñandutí lace, a kind of needlework distinguished by its intricate and fragile designs, exemplifies the essence of Paraguayan artistic expression. The complex craftsmanship of lacework transcends its status as a simple art form, as it serves as a medium for narrative expression, whereby threads are skillfully interwoven to convey stories including themes of love, nature, and historical events. Observing the genesis of ñandutí lace or actively participating in seminars dedicated to its practice gives individuals the opportunity to establish a connection with the craft's historical heritage and cultivate an enhanced admiration for the dexterity and perseverance required to produce each intricate masterpiece.

In a same vein, ao po'i textiles serve as an additional manifestation of Paraguay's rich creative legacy. These textiles are meticulously crafted via intergenerational knowledge transfer, using traditional handweaving processes. They exhibit a rich array of vivid hues and intricate geometric motifs, serving as a visual representation of the diverse cultural heritage of the country. The act of investigating various marketplaces and actively interacting with skilled craftsmen presents a valuable prospect to get these elaborate creations and gain a comprehensive comprehension of their cultural importance.

Religious festivals and rituals have a significant role in fostering faith and promoting cultural unity.

The religious composition of Paraguay exhibits a synthesis of indigenous spiritual practices and Catholicism, which emerged as a consequence of the amalgamation of belief systems during the colonial era. Religious festivals and rites have a significant position within the cultural calendar, serving as a means for communities to manifest their religious beliefs and commemorate their cultural heritage.

Semana Santa, often known as Holy Week, serves as a dramatic illustration of this amalgamation of cultures. The Paraguayan population participates in the commemoration of the Passion of Christ by means of processions, reenactments, and ceremonies that intricately blend Catholic observances with indigenous traditions. The phenomenon of spiritual convergence serves to highlight the nation's capacity to reconcile and integrate various cultural and ideological influences, so establishing a collective consciousness and a common cultural legacy among its populace.

4. Culinary Traditions: An Exploration of Historical and Contemporary Gastronomy

The culinary traditions of Paraguay exemplify the harmonious amalgamation of indigenous and European elements, giving rise to a diverse range of tastes that have significance in terms of historical and cultural contexts. Chipa, a highly esteemed bread prepared from manioc flour, has significance not just as a gastronomic pleasure but also as a representation of communal meetings and festive occasions. The production of chipa and the accompanying ceremonies serve as a prime illustration of the amalgamation of cultural heritage and gastronomic craftsmanship.

Another notable culinary delicacy is sopa paraguaya, a traditional meal consisting of cornbread and cheese that provides a soothing and nostalgic flavor reminiscent of Paraguayan households. Engaging in the process of preparing and communally partaking in this culinary creation with the indigenous populace throughout one's sojourn offers a unique opportunity to gain insight into the essence of Paraguayan culture. In this context, gastronomy assumes a significant role as a conduit that connects historical traditions with contemporary practices.

The topic of indigenous communities and their relationship with the land is of great significance.

The indigenous people of Paraguay play a crucial and vital role in the preservation of the country's cultural variety and environmental sustainability. From the Chaco Region to the core of Ybycuí National Park, these villages have preserved their traditional ways of life, showcasing a great reverence for the environment and a profound connection with the territory.

Participating in these communities provides an opportunity to acquire knowledge from their accumulated expertise, as they generously impart their customs, narratives, and methodologies. Engaging in routine practices, such as fishing, farming, or making, affords individuals a direct encounter with their symbiotic rapport with the natural surroundings.

6. Cultural Significance of Musical Heritage: Exploring the Essence of Rhythms

The musical legacy of Paraguay is evident in the emotive melodies produced by instruments such as the harp, guitar, and indigenous musical apparatus. The polka and guarania are representative musical genres that encapsulate narratives of love, historical events, and the human condition. The universal nature of music enables it to transcend linguistic boundaries, facilitating a profound connection between listeners and the many emotions and storylines embedded within its melodic fabric.

Participating in live presentations of traditional Paraguayan music provides an opportunity to engage with and contribute to the rich musical heritage of this cultural tradition. Observing proficient musicians deftly manipulating the strings of the harp or guitar elicits a profound appreciation for the historical legacy and lasting cultural manifestations of the country.

The examination of Paraguay's cultural insights reveals a country in which time-honored customs coexist harmoniously with modern existence, where the commemoration of indigenous legacy occurs alongside the impact of colonialism, and where the safeguarding of cultural identity is a collective undertaking. By actively engaging with Guarani communities, seeing the meticulous craftsmanship, actively participating in religious events, appreciating the culinary delicacies, and immersing oneself in Paraguay's rich musical legacy, one may establish a profound connection with a nation that both cherishes its historical roots and accepts contemporary developments. The exploration of cultural variety in Paraguay serves as evidence of the country's ability to endure and its dedication to incorporating elements of its legacy into a dynamic and captivating narrative that continues to attract and engage global tourists.

CHAPTER 6

Paraguay's Accommodation

When embarking on a voyage through Paraguay, a nation abundant in cultural opulence and breathtaking natural marvels, the selection of lodging may significantly shape one's trip encounter. Paraguay has a wide array of lodging alternatives that appeal to varied interests and enrich the discovery of the nation's distinctive tapestry. These possibilities include attractive boutique hotels, eco-friendly lodges, and traditional homestays. Paraguay's accommodations provide more than just lodging, as they serve as gates to real experiences that deeply connect with the essence of the country. Whether one seeks comfort, cultural immersion, or a harmonic combination of both, these accommodations provide opportunities for meaningful engagement.

1. The Significance of Boutique Hotels in Providing Cultural Comfort

Paraguay's boutique hotels provide a seamless fusion of contemporary conveniences and authentic cultural immersion, catering to discerning guests who value both comfort and cultural involvement. These enterprises often inhabit ancient structures that have been meticulously renovated, giving individuals the opportunity to immerse themselves in the past while also indulging in modern amenities.

In the capital city of Asunción, boutique hotels provide an opportunity to get insight into Paraguay's colonial heritage. One may find oneself living inside a meticulously restored home, whose each nook and cranny serves as a testament to bygone eras. The tastefully appointed accommodations, embellished with indigenous artwork and decorations, provide an ambiance that commemorates the cultural wealth of Paraguay.

2. Eco-Friendly Lodges: Embracing Nature's Sustainability

The varied topography of Paraguay, with lush woods and expansive grasslands, presents an appealing destination for environmentally minded tourists. One may promote sustainable tourism by selecting environmentally conscious accommodations that harmoniously integrate with their natural surroundings and provide immersive opportunities to engage with the environment.

The lodges situated in the central region of Ybycuí National Park provide a unique and unequalled chance for individuals to establish a profound connection with the surrounding natural environment. Experience the awakening of nature via the melodious symphony of avian vocalizations, engage in expertly led excursions through verdant pathways, and immerse yourself in the celestial spectacle of the nocturnal firmament. These lodges often place emphasis on implementing environmentally sustainable techniques, so guaranteeing that your accommodation supports the conservation of Paraguay's natural resources.

3. Homestays: Cultural Exchange via Tradition Sharing

For those who are interested in immersing themselves in authentic cultural encounters, the option of engaging in homestays with indigenous people offers a unique opportunity to get insights into their everyday routines and cultural practices. The Chaco Region, renowned for its indigenous populations like as the Enxet and Ayoreo, presents a unique prospect for individuals to live among these communities and acquire valuable perspectives on their cultural practices.

Engage in fishing, farming, and crafting endeavors while fully immersing oneself in the associated cultural practices. The homestays serve as more than just accommodations, as they provide opportunities for individuals to gain insights into the interrelationships of individuals, cultures, and the environment. Engaging in communal dining experiences and exchanging narratives with one's hosts cultivates a sense of mutual comprehension and a deepened admiration for the time-honored knowledge that shapes their way of life.

4. Luxury Resorts: An Exquisite Haven

Paraguay offers a selection of upscale resorts that appeal to the desires of discerning guests in search of optimal comfort and delight. These luxurious accommodations include top-tier facilities, wellness services, and high-quality culinary offerings, guaranteeing a luxury sojourn that enhances your discovery of the nation's points of interest.

Certain luxury resorts in Paraguay are strategically situated in close proximity to natural beauties, therefore offering a harmonious integration of leisure and exploration. Envision the act of relaxing in a secluded villa, situated within verdant environs, subsequent to a day spent visiting cascades, rainforests, or locations of historical significance.

5. Affordable Accommodations: Traveler's Haven In this section, we will discuss Traveler's Haven, a lodging option that offers budget-friendly accommodations for travelers.

The budget-friendly lodgings in Paraguay are specifically designed to cater to the requirements of guests who prioritize price while ensuring a satisfactory level of comfort. Hostels and guesthouses situated in metropolitan locales such as Asunción provide a congenial ambiance that facilitates social interaction among sojourners, fostering the exchange of narratives and experiences.

These lodgings often function as centers for cultural interchange, providing information on regional events, tourism, and recreational pursuits. These accommodations are well-suited for those who prioritize genuine experiences and want to optimize their time while adhering to financial constraints.

In this section, we will explore the cultural insights that may be gained via the practice of accommodation.

The lodgings selected in Paraguay serve as more than just lodging facilities, but rather serve as portals to get valuable cultural knowledge. The selection of accommodations in Paraguay offers many opportunities for visitors to deepen their knowledge of the country's character. Whether one opts for a homestay experience with a traditional Guarani meal, a boutique hotel showcasing colonial architecture, or an eco-friendly lodge emphasizing sustainable practices, each decision adds to a holistic exploration of Paraguay's cultural and environmental heritage.

By selecting lodging options that stress cultural involvement, individuals are able to actively participate in the story of the country. The encounters that individuals have with hosts, other travelers, and the local community serve to intertwine narratives that surpass geographical boundaries and provide light on the collective human experience.

The lodgings in Paraguay serve as a medium through which one's trip experiences are expressed and manifested. With a range of accommodations available, including luxury resorts and budget-friendly guesthouses, each choice provides a unique perspective for seeing the rich culture, historical heritage, and breathtaking natural landscapes of the country. Paraguay's hotels provide a diverse range of experiences, catering to those seeking either a peaceful escape or an enriching cultural immersion. These lodging options aim to transform your vacation from a mere sequence of locations into a collection of meaningful moments that leave a lasting impact and evoke enduring memories.

THE END

Printed in Dunstable, United Kingdom

63430723R00037